KEEP TALKING

DAILY CONVERSATION STARTERS FOR THE FAMILY MEAL

Maureen Treacy Lahr and Julie Pfitzinger

Liguori

LIGUORI, MISSOURI

Imprimi Potest: Thomas D. Picton, C.Ss.R. • Provincial, Denver Province • The Redemptorists
Published by Liguori Publications • Liguori, Missouri • www.liguori.org

Previously published under the same title by Beaver's Pond Press, Inc., Edina, Minnesota, 2003.

Library of Congress Cataloging-in-Publication Data

Lahr, Maureen Treacy.
    Keep talking : daily conversation starters for the family meal / Maureen Treacy Lahr, Julie Pfitzinger.—
Rev. ed.
      p.   cm.
   ISBN 0-7648-1307-2
    1. Communication in the family—Miscellanea. 2. Parent and child—Miscellanea. 3. Dinners and dining—Miscellanea. I. Pfitzinger. Julie. II. Title.

HQ734.L18 2005
306.87—dc22   2005043579

09 08 07 06 05 5 4 3 2 1
Revised edition 2005

*In loving memory
of Bill and Terry Treacy,
who encouraged family
conversations nightly around
the dinner table with
their ten children.*

Introduction

A child's first words are a true milestone for parents. From a baby's simple expression of names for familiar objects to exuberant toddler chatter to the never-ending questions of a preschooler, our children's ability to converse with us is nothing less than a precious gift. Words open a window into their minds and hearts. As parents, these early conversations provide us with wonderful opportunities to teach and to share ideas.

As children get older, our conversations with them often lack the joy of those first discussions and now we're the ones asking the endless questions: Did you clean your room? Did you finish your homework? Will you stop teasing your sister?

If this sounds like the type of "conversation" you routinely have with your kids, you're not alone. The busyness of today's world often forces us to check off topics on a mental "to do" list instead of taking time to engage our children in genuine, open, and caring dialogue.

One of the easiest places to have a good family conversation is around the

dinner table. For generations, families passed the potatoes and offered opinions about topics such as politics, religion, values, family concerns, almost anything. But today's families find that gathering everyone around the dinner table each night is not an easy task. There are so many demands on our time as parents, and unfortunately, the commitments that many of our children have to sports, music lessons, and other extracurricular activities often result in scattered snacks and drive-though meals.

Studies reveal that it is in our best interest to once again make family mealtime a priority. While clearly benefitting children of all ages, a dinnertime ritual can be especially important for adolescents. A Columbia University study found that teenagers who ate dinner with their families on a regular basis were less likely to smoke, drink, or use illegal drugs. By routinely gathering together for meals, families have the opportunity to engage with one another in many ways that can result in improved parenting and healthier children.

Family time is a precious commodity. We encourage you to enjoy the simple pleasures in life such as a meal shared around the table. Time spent together as a family is time meant to be cherished.

Suggested Guidelines

It is our hope that *Keep Talking: Daily Conversation Starters for the Family Meal* will help enhance your own family's mealtime ritual.

- Place this book on or near your dinner table and use it often. Questions are on both sides of each page.
- Listen to how your children respond to the questions and look for teachable moments. This is also a good opportunity to help family members learn to articulate their thoughts aloud.
- You may find it helpful to adjust a question slightly to make it more age appropriate for the respondent.
- Reflect on comments that may generate broader discussion at another time.
- Defer judgment. Listen to the full response without evaluating it prematurely.
- Allow the kids to come up with their own questions or "what ifs" occasionally.

If you expected to win the election for student council president, but didn't, would it be hard for you to congratulate the winner? Why?

Keep Talking!

How would you feel if someone threw a surprise party for you?

Your basketball coach lets his child play most of the game, which means you have to sit on the bench more even though you are about equal in ability. How do you handle the situation?

Keep Talking!

If your dog could talk, what kind of voice would she have? What would your dog say to you? How would she describe living with your family?

Keep Talking!

If you were given a hundred dollars to spend on anyone EXCEPT yourself, who would you spend it on and what would you buy?

Think of a time when you were laughing so hard you couldn't stop. Describe what was so funny!

Have you ever visited someone in the hospital? If so, what do you remember most about it? If not, what do you think it would be like?

If you could change places
with someone for one day,
who would it be and why would
you choose that person?

What does being "popular" mean to you? Is it important to you, and if it is, why?

Describe your favorite family photo. Why is it your favorite?

Name your top three favorite mothers other than your own. Why are they your favorites?

What is the strangest dream
you've ever had?
What's the silliest? The scariest?

Name three of your favorite qualities about one of your sisters or brothers.

Describe the most embarrassing moment of your life.

Glue has been squirted into the lockers. The junior high dance will be canceled if the person(s) involved are not identified. Your best friend tells you who did it. What do you do?

Keep Talking!

If you are eating dinner at a friend's house and they serve food you don't like, what do you do?

If you could do one thing over and change the outcome, what would it be?

What do you think your parents would say are the top five reasons for having children?

Someone describes what you would do if your home smoke detector went off in the middle of the night. How does your answer change if you were staying at a hotel and the smoke detector went off?

Keep Talking!

What does it feel like when you're in a good mood? What does it feel like when you're in a bad mood?

You've just learned that a class-mate's mother is very ill. What kind of things would you consider doing to help? How is your answer different if it were your best friend's mother?

Ask the oldest person at the table to describe one of his/her favorite childhood memories. Ask the

youngest person at the table to describe one of his/her favorite childhood memories!

You know someone who often tells lies or exaggerates stories. Why do you think he does this? When you know something he says is a lie, do you correct him or let it go?

Keep Talking!

If you could choose between being a doctor, a pilot, or a movie star, which would you pick? Why?

What is your biggest fear? Think about a time when you felt truly brave and describe the experience.

What is your all-time favorite...
A chore to do around the house?
Flavor of ice cream?
Birthday present? Green vegetable?

What does it mean to feel "peaceful"? When have you felt that way in your life?

If you were a superhero, what would your power be and what would you call yourself?

How important is family time to you? To your parents? Name your three favorite family activities. Name an activity your family has never tried that you think you all would enjoy.

"There is nothing small in the service of God" (Saint Francis de Sales). What is one thing you can do this week to serve God?

Keep Talking!

Has someone you counted on ever disappointed you? Think of a time when you know you disappointed another person. How did you resolve the situation?

Keep Talking!

If you were a veterinarian and knew a family's dog had no chance of survival but they insisted you treat it, how would you handle the situation?

When you go to an amusement park, do you head for the thrilling rides or prefer the mild ones?

If God came to eat dinner with your family, what would you talk about?

If you could rename yourself, what name would you choose?

If each of the following pairs were combined into one animal, what sound do you think it would make:

A dog and a bird?

A duck and a horse?

A frog and an elephant?

How much do you think your parents' first car cost? What do you think the average car costs today? When do you think you'll get your first car? How will you pay for it?

At a party everyone is playing "truth or dare." The group dares you to replace the money in the younger brother's piggy bank with a handful of pennies and split his quarters with the partygoers. Do you?

Keep Talking!

If the meal you ordered at a restaurant is not prepared the way you like it, do you eat it or ask for it to be redone?

Do you like being with people who act a little daring and out of the ordinary? Why?

Spend time describing a typical day in the year 1897. Think about life without electricity or indoor water and toilets. What food would you prepare? How would you wash your clothes?

Keep Talking!

If a parent gives a punishment as a consequence for something a child has done wrong then does not follow through on the punishment, what does the child learn?

Keep Talking!

If your family is stopped at a red light and you see an unshaven, unclean man holding a sign asking to work for food, do you think your family should stop and offer him something? Why?

If someone plays a joke on you
at school and others laugh,
do you laugh along with them
or get angry? Why?

"If you're too busy to pray, you're too busy" (Unknown). Do you think there's such a thing as being too busy to pray? When are some times during the day when you could pray?

How do you respond when someone gives you a compliment?

If someone sitting next to you was smoking and it bothered you, would you ask the person to stop or would you move?

Which parent do you think you act most like? Why?

When you know you've hurt someone else's feelings, how does that make you feel? What about when you've hurt someone on purpose?

Keep Talking!

The church youth group's service trip to Appalachia is scheduled for the same week as your family's annual vacation. Which trip would you go on and why?

Have you ever seen a parent or a close adult friend cry? Do you try to hold in your own feelings so others won't see you cry? Why or why not?

You and your friend recently turned thirteen. At a restaurant with your friend and his parents, it is "kids twelve and under eat free." To get two free meals, your friend's parent says you are both twelve. Do you say anything?

Keep Talking!

A true friend is a gift.
Name some of your favorite things
about one of your true friends.

Name your favorite teacher of all time. Why was he/she your favorite?

You auditioned for a lead part in the school play. The next day you learned one of your close friends got the part instead. How do you handle the situation?

Describe the most exciting moment of your life so far!

While helping at your school carnival's fishpond a group of your sixth-grade friends cut in front of a kindergartner who's been waiting in line. The little girl doesn't seem to mind, but what do you say when your friends ask for a turn?

Keep Talking!

If you could do just one thing to change the world, what would it be?

If you knew a friend is afraid of dogs, would you move your dog to another room when he comes to visit or would you try to convince him that she's a gentle dog?

How would you describe the state of your bedroom on most days—tidy, a hurricane zone, or organized chaos? Do you think your parents are pleased with the way you keep your room? Why?

Keep Talking!

Did you ever have trouble forgiving a friend who has done something to hurt you? Why, and how have you come to forgive her?

**Describe what you think
your life will be like in five years,
ten years, and fifteen years.**

Would you rather spend your free time alone or with others?

A classmate gets on the school bus and says, "I watched the baseball game last night and didn't have time to do my math homework.

Will you let me copy your answers on the way to school?" How do you respond?

Name three things that you would like to improve about yourself.

"God loves each of us
as if there were only one of us"
(Saint Augustine).
How has God shown love
for you today?

Do you ever feel lonely? Describe what it means to feel lonely. How do you get past the feeling? How can you help others feel less lonely?

Name a well-known hero.

Is there a hero in your own life?

What makes that person a hero for you?

At a school dance your best friend is talking to a different group of kids. When you approach the group your friend ignores you. How do you react?

Keep Talking!

People often pray when they have big problems. Can you think of other good reasons for people to pray?

What has been the happiest day of your life?

Would you rather spend a week in an igloo or a week in a rain forest? Why?

**Describe your "dream job"
in detail.**

How would you define "rich"?

Do you feel like you have enough free time in a week? Or do you feel you have too much to do? Why?

Name three things you are thankful for today.

What benefits do you think graduating from college could bring you?

Grandma is getting to the point where she cannot take care of herself or live on her own anymore.

How does your family go about deciding how to help Grandma?

What do you think it means to be holy and to live a holy life? Can you think of some examples of holy people?

If you want something very much, do you usually find a way to get it? How?

Describe what you think heaven might be like.

If you were put in charge of dinner for a night, what would you make? How do you make it?

Do you think parents should go out on dates without their children? Why?

You are sixteen. All your friends are going to an R-rated movie. Your family rule is that you cannot go to an R-rated movie until you are seventeen. What do you do when your friends ask you to go to the movie?

Keep Talking!

"What you are is God's gift to you; what you make of it is your gift to God." What does this mean to you? What are some of your gifts that are meant to be shared with others?

Keep Talking!

Complete the sentence,
"My family is _____."

Describe something that happened this week that made you mindful of your faith.

You have to give an oral book report in two days, but you've run out of time to read. You can buy a book summary at the local bookstore.

Keep Talking!

book summary at the local bookstore. What would you do to prepare for the book report?

Do you think it is fair for a teacher to make everyone stay in from recess because someone put a "Kick Me" sticker on a classmate's back, which caused the whole class to laugh when he turned around?

At camp, your roommates start saying bad things about your best friend who is not at camp. Do you say anything?

If you could ask God one question, what would it be?

List ten things you could do instead of watching TV or playing computer and video games.

Every family goes through difficult times. Can suffering be seen in a positive way? Do we gain anything from suffering?

When your group of friends is trying to make a decision—say about what movie to see—do you typically speak up and make suggestions or just go along with what the group decides?

Keep Talking!

If your group of buddies is giving you a hard time one day, how do you react? If they tease you more and more over time, would you speak up or move to another group?

While volunteering at a nursing home, you've befriended a lonely, ill man who wants you to pray that he'll die soon. Are you comfortable praying for someone to die? Why or why not?

For each of the following words, what smell comes to mind: school, church, Grandma's house, Thanksgiving?

You meet a person in a wheelchair on a hilly street who asks you for directions to the local store, what information do you need to consider before giving the person directions?

How many hours a day are you in front of electronic devices (computers, TV, video games)? How many hours a day are you outside or playing with friends?

You do not smoke cigarettes, but your fifteen-year-old friend asks to borrow money to buy cigarettes. What do you think about when considering whether to lend the money or not?

What qualities do you look for in a friend? Do you have those same qualities?

Describe your soul.
What happens to your soul
when you die?

**If you could create a new law,
what would it be about and why?**

What are some favorite memories of the way your family celebrates faith traditions and rituals?

**Invite everyone at the table
to share a favorite memory
of a family member who has died.**

Have you prayed for someone today? For who, and why?

If you could turn your life into a TV show, what type of show would it be? What song would you pick for the theme song?

Keep Talking!

Your family just received $400 from Aunt Edna. Which of the following ways would you choose to use her gift: go on a shopping spree, fix the car, save it, donate it to charity?

Keep Talking!

When a child is really angry with her parents, how can she tell her parents about that anger?

If classmates constantly ridicule a student, how would you feel if the teacher steps in to defend her?

Each of you is asked to eliminate one of your activities. What would you eliminate and why? What would you do as a family with the additional time?

Keep Talking!

What should a parent do to a fifteen-year-old who takes the key to the car and goes on a joy ride? Would your answer differ if the police stopped the teenager?

Keep Talking!

How do you think Sunday should differ from the other days of the week?

When you think of a job or career, do you think you'd like to do the same thing your mom or dad does? Why or why not?

What puts you in a bad mood? Name your three favorite ways to "snap out" of a bad mood.

If there were one food you could eat every day of your life, what would it be? Name one food that you'd just as soon never have again. Name one food that you'd like to try but never have.

Keep Talking!

What does it mean to have respect for someone? Name two people you have respect for and explain why.

You're nine and visiting a friend and his sixteen-year-old sister is in charge. She chooses a PG-13 movie for all of you to watch, but you know your parents don't allow you to watch PG-13 movies. What do you do?

Keep Talking!

When is the last time you sent a letter (not an e-mail) to someone? If it's been awhile, set aside a few minutes after dinner to write a letter to a friend or relative.

Parents: Do your children remind you of the way you were when you were young? How are they the same? How are they different?

Keep Talking!

Name the country you'd most like to visit and why. Have you ever thought of going to school in a foreign country? What do you think that would be like?

Keep Talking!

Describe something that happened at school this week that you didn't think was "fair." Why did you feel this way?

Keep Talking!

You are preparing for confirmation and you are required to do a service project in your community. What kinds of things would you consider doing? How will you accumulate service hours for this project?

Keep Talking!

If your teacher assigns a really big project, how much, if any, help should you ask your parents to give you?

If you see a person with a disability struggling to maneuver around a corner, do you ask if she needs help or wait to see if she asks for help?
Why?

Keep Talking!

Your locker is next to a student who smells of marijuana. In addition, you see packets of marijuana in her locker. Do you ignore this or alert a teacher? If you choose to discuss it with a teacher, how do you do it?

Keep Talking!

What do you think is the easiest part about being a teacher? What do you think is the hardest part?

Keep Talking!

What do you worry about?
Why does that make you worry?
What do you do when you feel
worried about something?

Keep Talking!

Describe your "dream house" in detail.

If you could be the creator, would you create both good and evil? Why?

Keep Talking!

If the nightly news is reporting a terrible disaster, are you drawn to the television or do you avoid it? Why?

You have a test tomorrow in history and you haven't studied much for it. Your sister still has her old test, which is probably the same one the teacher will give to your class. Would you consider using that old test to study for your test?

Keep Talking!

What do you think is the hardest part about being an adult? What do you think is the easiest part?

A friend of yours is always admiring your autographed baseball. The day after he and a few other friends

were at your house, you discover the ball is missing. How do you go about finding out where the ball is?

If you were given $1,000 to eat five chocolate-covered raw caterpillars, would you? Why?

Think of a time when you felt really proud of yourself. Why did you feel this way and did you have a good reason to feel proud?

Name your worst habit.
Think of three ways you can work
on breaking it or developing
a better habit.

Describe your favorite character from a book. What qualities does that person have that you like? If you could be a character in your

favorite book, who would you be and why?

Someday you might have your own grandchildren. What will you tell them about what life was like for you when you were a child?

What is your favorite prayer? Say it now and then tell why it's your favorite.

What does it mean to be humble? Give an example.

Describe three qualities about yourself.

You are baby-sitting for a family that lives five miles away. The couple comes home and appears goofy, like they have had too much to drink. The dad is about to drive you home. What do you do?

Do you prefer one or two close friends or would you rather be part of a bigger group? Why?

How do you feel when someone you're playing with on a team does really well and gets recognized for it even though you feel you did just as well?

Your parents have given you and your sister the chance to choose the family's vacation—an amusement park or a trip to the mountains. What if she doesn't choose the same place as you do? How will your family decide?

If you could change one thing about your neighborhood, what would it be and why?

A couple of your buddies have started daring another friend to do some naughty things. The friend seems to enjoy getting the attention.

What would you do if you thought this behavior was getting out of control or unsafe?

Why do you think it's sometimes hard to apologize to another person for something you've done wrong?

Describe your "perfect" day. Describe what you think would be your mom or dad's "perfect" day. How is this description the same or different from yours?

Are you better at saving money or spending money? Why?

A classmate annoys you and your friends but you can tolerate her at school. On the weekends she calls you to do things socially, but you

do not want to include her. How do you handle the situation?

Describe the type of transportation you think people will be using in fifty years. How about one hundred years?

If you have brothers or sisters, what are your favorite things to do together?

"Honesty is the best policy."
What does that mean and why do
you think it's true? Think about
a time when someone
didn't tell you the
truth—how did
that make you feel?

Keep Talking!

When was the last time you volunteered to help someone without being asked? There are many different ways to volunteer your time to help others. Choose one activity to volunteer for during the next week.

Keep Talking!

How do you feel when you see a classmate being mean to someone? Are there things you can do to be helpful in this kind of situation?

Your friends are trying to talk you into dyeing your hair orange. What things would you consider before deciding to change your hair color?

Do you think you will hire a cleaning service to clean your house when you grow up or have family members share the responsibility? Why?

Keep Talking!

Whenever you play at a certain friend's house, the friend is mean when the two of you are alone. He's suddenly very nice when his mom comes in the room. What do you do?

Keep Talking!

If you could ask for one miracle, what would it be?

If you could live anywhere in the world? Where would you live? Why?

List three safety rules you need to follow if you're home alone after school.

What's your favorite photo of yourself when you were a baby? What were you doing in the picture? There are lots of ways you look different, but are there any ways you still look the same?

"Trust in God but tie your camel" (Persian Proverb). This is a funny idea, but there is truth in it. What do you think it means?

Everyone has a bad day every once in a while. Describe one of your most recent bad days.

If you were a cat, what would you think about during the day?
Do you think cats have a sense of humor?

Your parents will let you buy a new video game if you pay for half of it. Your cousin offers to give it to you, saying she'll just borrow it from her parents' dresser. Do you consider taking the money?

Keep Talking!

**How can you show love
to your family or friends
through your daily actions?**

If you could have anyone sitting at your dinner table right now, who would it be and why?

**If you could be the president
of the United States for one day,
what would you do?**

"Do unto others as you would have them do unto you." What do you think this means? This expression is known as the golden rule. Why?

Do you know a funny joke?
Tell it now! What if you know a
hilarious joke that is inappropriate,
do you tell it?

If you were given $100 to spend on yourself, what would you do with the money?

You used to love to play soccer, but your new league is more competi- tive, which has made you anxious and worried about playing this year. Your parents want you to stick with it. What do you do?

List three safety rules you need to follow when you're riding your bike around the neighborhood.

You are shopping with a friend who has found an outfit she loves, but you think it is not very flattering. What do you say when she asks your opinion?

Keep Talking!

If you could live in any time in the past, what time period would you choose? Describe what you think it would be like to live in that time period.

What do you think it would be like to travel in outer space?
What would be the most fun?
Do you think it would be scary?

Do you think you spend time helping others? What kinds of things do you do?

If you could change one thing about your bedroom, what would it be?

Do you think the world would be a happier place if everyone had the same beliefs and opinions? Why?

After you have made a decision, do you stick with it or can you be easily convinced to change your mind?

Smoking is not allowed at your school, but you've noticed one of the rest rooms is often filled with smoke during the day. Do you mention something to a teacher or do you just use another rest room?

How would a friend describe you?

You have injured your knee during gymnastics. The doctor advises you to rest for three weeks. After two weeks your knee is only a little sore. Do you rejoin the team to participate in the champion-ship or wait?

Keep Talking!

If you're working on a group project in school and something goes wrong, how do you react?

We often hear about becoming successful. How would you define success?

If you are at a movie and the people in front of you are making noise, what do you do?

List three safety rules you need to follow if you're at the shopping mall with friends.

Do you think there are situations when it is better not to be totally honest?
Describe those situations.

When you have a point of view that is different from a friend's, how do you go about trying to understand his point of view?

If you could, would you go on an African safari? Why?

**If you saw an injured bird
in your yard, what would you do?**

Have you ever asked an older relative what life was like when he was your age? What is the most interesting thing he shared with you about that time? If you haven't asked, make time to talk to someone soon.

Keep Talking!

What makes you angry?
What's the best way
to let someone know you're mad?

What does it mean to be organized? Do you consider yourself an organized person? If not, how can you become more organized?

Is there something you used to be afraid of that you're not afraid of anymore? What changed that made you stop being afraid?

Keep Talking!

You are playing alone in your yard and a man in a car pulls up to ask for directions to the nearest fast-food restaurant. What do you do?

What do you like and/or dislike about speaking in front of a group of people?

What do you enjoy most about being on a team? What is your least favorite thing about being on a team?

If you had an opportunity
to parachute from a plane,
would you?

"Patience is a virtue." Do you know what that expression means? Why is it important to have patience? Think of a time when you had to be patient and describe those feelings.

Keep Talking!

Where did you see God today?

If you could change one thing
about your school,
what would it be?

If you get lost, would you continue to try to figure out the way using a map or stop and ask for directions?

How do you react when someone cuts in front of you when you are waiting in line for concert tickets that are sure to sell out quickly?

If you were in an elevator with a stranger, traveling to the twenty-fourth floor, would you start a conversation?

Do you think school is different today than it was when your parents were students? Why or why not? Parents, do you think today's schools are different?

**Describe your "dream vacation"
in detail.**

**What is the best thing about
the first day of school?**

If you could create a movie that would portray the life you hope to lead, describe the movie.

What do you think is the hardest part about being a doctor? Why?

Name the top three reasons to get married.

What would you do if you were given an entire day to be alone?

If your parents were asked to use
three words to describe you,
what words do you think
they would choose?

If you were asked to place your favorite outfit in a time capsule, what would you choose?

Do you find it difficult to stick with a project that is challenging? Have you ever given up on something because it was too hard to complete? How did that make you feel?

If you had really bad service at a restaurant, which family member do you think would say something to the manager?

When you have an argument with one of your parents, how do you feel after it's over? Who is usually the first one to apologize or try to smooth things over?

You know you have a lot of home-work to do, but your best friend who lives down the street doesn't have any and he wants you to come over and play video games. What do you do?

Your new neighbor asks you to baby-sit on Friday night and you say yes. At school, you find out a friend is having a party the same night. What do you do?

While in class, your chair accidentally tips over, which disrupts the classroom. Your teacher accuses you of doing it on purpose to attract attention, but you know that's not true. What do you do?

Keep Talking!

You've just started a new school and are beginning to make friends. A former classmate from your old school seems to be having a hard time in the new school. How can you help?

What does it mean to be a good person? Think of some examples of good people you know.

**What's the best thing
about the last day of school?
What's the worst thing about it?**

If you could be a cartoon character, who would you be and why?

Imagine yourself as a seventy-five-year-old person. What do you think you will look like? If you could ask that older version of yourself one question, what would it be?

What does it mean to be proud?
What does it mean to be humble?
Is one of these traits better than
the other? Why?

How would you feel about eating alone at a restaurant? Would you feel like you needed to do something while you waited for your food?

If you find your mind wanders when you pray, do you continue praying?

Do you have any fears about going to the doctor? What are they?

Describe a culture other than your own. Would you like to live in this culture?

Describe what you are least likely to do.

You are going to go to work at the candy factory with one of your parents for a day. Who do you expect to see working the hardest— the owner, the managers, or the candy makers? Why?

What is your favorite time of day? Why?

At the school lunch table, you sit with the same friends every day. One day you notice a classmate sitting alone. What do you do?

You follow the instructions to build a birdhouse, but it is not turning out the way it looks on the box. How do you react?

What books will you pick to read during your next vacation?

Do you typically fall asleep quickly
or toss and turn for a while?
If you toss and turn,
what helps you
get to sleep?

How do you decide what music you listen to? Has anyone influenced your music choices?

As you walk down the street, a stranger at the corner says something rude to you. What do you say?

Do you usually like a lot of activity around you or do you prefer a peaceful atmosphere? Why?

Would you sing in front of a group of strangers? Would your answer be different if you knew people in the group?

What movie has touched you deeply? Describe a favorite scene from the movie.

If you and your family are stuck in a traffic jam, what kinds of things could you do to pass the time?

If your school was holding tryouts for a play, would you go for a lead part, the chorus, or the stage crew? Why?

Name your top three fathers other than your own. Why are they your favorites?

What section of the newspaper do you read first? Why do you go for that section?

What is your favorite season? Why?

Imagine you are a chef and describe a special dish you would create to serve in your restaurant.

**Think of one of your best friends.
Do you think you'll still be close
ten years from now?
Why or why not?**

Parents: Who is the friend you've had for the longest time? How has your friendship changed over the years?

What is your favorite possession?
How important do you think
it will be to you in ten years?
In twenty years?

If you could go on a trip with a grandparent or older relative, where would you go and why?

How would you describe the members of your family to someone who's never met them before?

Which animal do you think is the "coolest" one in all of creation, and why do you think so?

If you could be a red cardinal for one day, where would you fly?

Parents: Have you ended up with the job or career you planned to have? If not, what did you want to

be when you were younger? How would your life be different if you had that job instead of the one you have?

If you could spend a week alone in a forest or on a deserted island, which would you choose and why?

If you could walk across America, would you do it? Why or why not?

How would you describe your best friend to someone who's never met her before?

In the eyes of God, all people are important. How do you show people they are important to you?

When you go shopping with friends, do you usually buy something? Does it depend on whether the others buy anything?

Name one of your favorite popular musicians. Do you think you'll still be listening to his or her music in ten years?

Parents: What was your favorite band when you were younger? Do you still listen to their music today? Who is your favorite current popular musician?

Have you ever worried about a friend?

What do you think is the most beautiful part of nature?

If you live in the city, describe what you think would be the best part of living in the country. If you live in the country, what do you think is the best part of city living?

Have you ever been in a situation where you told the truth about something, but the other person

didn't believe you? How did that make you feel? Were you able to convince him that you were being truthful?

"The grass is always greener on the other side of the fence." What do you think that expression means? Have you ever felt that way about something?

If you could cure one disease, what would it be and why?

What is the best part about having dinner with your family?

About the Authors

Maureen Treacy Lahr has a background in marketing and project management in the insurance industry. She and her husband live in Mendota Heights, Minnesota, with their two teenage children.

Julie Pfitzinger is a freelance writer specializing in parenting and faith issues. She and her husband and two children live in West St. Paul, Minnesota.